2-80

CW00419143

How Someone Near You Who Is Away from God

JOY DAWSON

PUBLISHING

A Ministry Of Youth With A Mission

P.O. Box 55787, Seattle, WA 98155

YWAM Publishing is the publishing ministry of Youth With A Mission. Youth With A Mission (YWAM) is an international missionary organization of Christians from many denominations dedicated to presenting Jesus Christ to this generation. To this end, YWAM has focused its efforts in three main areas: 1) Training and equipping believers for their part in fulfilling the Great Commission (Matthew 28:19). 2) Personal evangelism. 3) Mercy ministry (medical and relief work).

For a free catalog of books and materials write or call:
YWAM Publishing
P.O. Box 55787, Seattle, WA 98155
(425) 771-1153 or (800) 922-2143
e-mail address: 75701.2772 @ compuserve.com

How to Pray for Someone Near You Who Is Away from God

ISBN 0-96155-347-2

Published by YWAM Publishing
P.O. Box 55787, Seattle, WA 98155, USA

Printed in the United States of America.

How to Pray for Someone Near You Who Is Away from God

After I had finished speaking at a church in Northern California, a woman introduced herself and her husband to me and told me the following story.

This woman had earnestly prayed for many years for her husband's conversion, always asking God to move upon her husband and motivate him to come to church with her. As a keen church member, she found much joy and fulfillment in being involved in the life and ministry of her vital church. A part of that vitality was that people were regularly committing their lives to the Lord Jesus Christ during services, and the woman repeatedly thought, "If only my husband would come to church, I *know* he would be converted." The woman was disappointed and very puzzled as to why her prayers were not being answered. Her husband chose not to go to church and remained unconverted.

The woman had taken home a number of taped messages that I had given at her church the previous year, and she enthusiastically told her husband about their contents—always hoping and praying that he would come to church and hear these truths for himself.

One day the woman's husband amazed her by announcing that he had totally given his life to the Lord Jesus while at home by himself. He had listened to a series of my taped messages on divine guidance—while she was attending church! He said he wanted to experience friendship and fulfillment with God as He was described on those tapes.

The woman's husband then testified to me of an exciting walk with the Lord on a daily basis—seeking Him, listening to His voice, and obeying Him. The major lesson the woman said she learned was that by dictating to God the method He should use to accomplish her husband's conversion (that is, attending church with her), she had unwittingly hindered the process.

My next statement has no connection with the woman to whom I have just referred. God has a special word of instruction to wives of unconverted husbands in 1 Peter 3:1. He emphasizes the power that is released to influence their husbands to become Christians through the Christlike *living* of their wives, as opposed to their repeated preaching.

PURITY OF MOTIVE

Another major hindrance to answered prayer when praying for someone we love who is away from God is having an impure motive. So many times, our main reason for wanting people to be converted is that life would be so much easier for us if they were Christians.

We need to ask God to purify our *motives* so that our requests for the souls of our loved ones to be saved come from a genuine, deep desire for God to be glorified to the maximum regardless of the cost to us, or to them. When we start praying that kind of prayer, we find we are soon tested. Those who understand God's character will pass the tests.

LESSONS WE NEED TO LEARN

As we submit to the Person of the Holy Spirit and obey His promptings, we will find that He puts the focus on us first. God wants us to say to Him, "What is it You are trying to teach me? I want to learn those lessons more than I want my circumstances to be changed."

We can then say, "If more glory can come to Your name by delaying the answers to my prayers, that's fine with me. Do whatever is needed in my life to bring me to the place where I have maximum effectiveness when I pray for those who are lost."

Now those are the people who mean business with God. And those are the people with whom God does business.

TOTAL RELINQUISHMENT

With a passionate desire for God to be glorified we will say with Paul, *"I eagerly expect and hope that I will in no way be ashamed, but will have sufficient courage so that now as always Christ will be exalted in my body, whether by life or by death"* (Philippians 1:20). We continue to say, "If by my death these unconverted people could be brought to You, I'm a candidate for death. Their soul's salvation means more to me than life." That is total relinquishment of oneself.

Then comes total relinquishment of the unconverted people, which also deals with selfish motives. We pray, "If more glory can come to Your name by Your bringing lost ones to You and then immediately taking them to heaven, that's also fine with me."

When we truly have a burdened heart for the lostness of people's souls, we will pray, "God, do anything that is required to bring them to the end of themselves—even if that means illness or injury, temporary or permanent." Are we prepared for these implications?

God both desires and has the power to bring us to the place where our desire for people to be in a right relationship with Him is greater than our desire for their—or our own—physical well-being.

Are we prepared to say to God, "Use anyone, anywhere, under any circumstances, to bring that lost soul to You"? Or have we prejudices (maybe hidden ones) about whom we would *not* want God to use?

We also need to relinquish the unconverted to God in relation to their future. We need to pray, "Lord, if after their conversion You should call them to a foreign mission field or they are martyred for You and I face the possibility of never seeing them again, that's okay. They're in Your hands for the present and the future."

TESTINGS RELATED TO GOD'S GLORY

We may have already said the foregoing to God but never really relinquished the people nearest and dearest to us into His hands, so that by their death, if necessary, God could use this to bring the unconverted to Himself. That's really where we know beyond a shadow of a doubt that we're praying one hundred percent for God's glory and have a God-given burden for the lost souls for whom we're praying. That's taking our Isaacs and laying them upon the altar on Mount Moriah. I know. I've been there! It's the ultimate test, because we know that God can take us at our word and we can be left widowed or childless or friendless or orphaned.

We can pray like this only if we understand the character of the One to whom we are praying. That understanding comes through studying God's character facet by facet from His Word, and being obedient to revealed truth.

God will never do anything inconsistent with His character. He is absolutely righteous and just, infinite in His knowledge and wisdom, unsearchable in His understanding, and unfathomable in His love. Because of *who He is* we can trust Him—to act according to the highest good for all concerned.

RELEASE FROM FEAR

We can fear dying ourselves, and we can fear our loved ones' dying. But when we really relinquish ourselves and our loved ones to God and truly want the greatest glory to come to His name through each of those lives, I can assure you that all fear leaves us, and God's peace takes its place.

If God decides to answer our prayers in the ways that we have released Him to, we can expect Him to do such wonderful things as a result of the people's conversions that the joy will outweigh the sorrow that has accompanied the sacrifice. *"The Lord is just in all his ways, and kind in all his doings"* (Psalm 145:17 RSV). We can also believe God to heal our broken heart and bind up our wounds (Psalm 147:3).

As we pass these tests by God's grace and with the understanding of His flawless character, not only are our motives for praying purified, but God brings us into closer friendship with Himself.

THE IMPORTANCE OF RIGHT ATTITUDES

The nearer we get to God, the more we become aware that our attitudes toward the people for whom we are praying are all-important for the further release of God's power through us. So often, the people whom we love but who are far away from God are those who have hurt us deeply. We need to make sure that we feel no resentment toward them as we pray for them. It is possible to pray fervently and for many years for people we have never forgiven. This is a major hindrance to our prayers being answered. *"See to it that no one misses the grace of God and that no bitter root grows up to cause trouble and defile many"* (Hebrews 12:15).

Perhaps we know the truth of this all too well, but still struggle to forgive. The following nine practical steps will produce sure forgiveness if diligently taken:

1. Realize that forgiveness is an act of the will. We have to want to forgive.

2. Understand that resentment is destructive to the mind, body, soul, and spirit. "A tranquil mind gives life to the flesh, but passion makes the bones rot" (Proverbs 14:30 RSV).

3. Realize that we will not be forgiven by God unless we forgive others who have hurt us. "And when you stand praying, if you hold anything against anyone, forgive him, so that your Father in heaven may forgive you your sins" (Mark 11:25).

4. Think of all that God has forgiven us. *"Be kind and compassionate to one another, forgiving each other, just as in Christ God forgave you"* (Ephesians 4:32); *"As the Lord has forgiven you,*

so you also must forgive" (Colossians 3:13b RSV). God forgives us instantly, joyfully, and wholly.

5. Thank the Lord for any or all of the blessings He has brought to us through the people who have hurt us.

6. Think of the needs—mental, physical, emotional, and spiritual—of the individuals at the time of their hurting us. Their needs then—and now—are probably greater than ours.

7. We ask God to give us His supernatural ability to love and forgive those people. Acknowledge that this is the work of the Holy Spirit and receive it by faith. "*God has poured out his love into our hearts by the Holy Spirit, whom he has given us*" (Romans 5:5b); "*And without faith, it is impossible to please God*" (Hebrews 11:6a). Galatians 5:6 says that "*faith [expresses] itself through love.*" And God has promised in 1 Corinthians 13:8a that "*love never fails.*"

8. We ask God for opportunities to express His love to these people both in word and in deed. "*If anyone has material possessions and sees his brother in need but has no pity on him, how can the love of God be in him? Dear children, let us not love with words or tongue but with actions and in truth*" (1 John 3:17-18).

9. Become a regular intercessor for them. Pray for God to bless them, encourage them, comfort them, strengthen them, and meet their deepest needs. "*But I tell you: Love your enemies and pray for those who persecute you*" (Matthew 5:44).

A dedicated Christian woman in California told me that after she had heard me speak on the subject of forgiveness, the Holy Spirit convicted her of her long-standing resentment toward her son-in-law.

Her son-in-law was unconverted, and for years had been cruel to her daughter and her grandchildren, causing her much sorrow. She had prayed fervently for years for his conversion, but without results.

That same night at 11:30 p.m., the woman knelt beside her bed and repented of her resentment. She then applied every one of the preceding nine steps as she realized the cause for the ineffectiveness of her prayers for her son-in-law's conversion. It was a Thursday night.

The following Saturday morning, her son-in-law unexpectedly burst into her house. He announced the startling news that at exactly 11:30 p.m. on the previous Thursday night he had felt a strong conviction of sin, had repented, and had given his life to Christ. He said that he had asked forgiveness of his wife and children and that he had felt compelled to drive to her home (although a long distance away) to ask for her forgiveness for all the heartache he had caused her. As soon as the woman had forgiven her son-in-law, God was able to answer her prayers.

RELEASE OF POWER THROUGH HUMBLING OURSELVES

We need to be encouraged that the more we let God work on us, the more the power of His Spirit will be released to work through us as we pray for the lost. Humbling ourselves before God and the people for whom we're praying is a strong factor in releasing that power.

We should ask God to show us any areas in our lives where we might have tempted the unconverted to rebel against Him. Even if we were ignorant of our doing so at the time, we still need to confess and make restitution as God directs.

It is also important to tell ourselves and them that we believe that God is greater in love, mercy, and power than our mistakes. *"Consecrate yourselves, for tomorrow the Lord will do amazing things among you"* (Joshua 3:5b).

So much of people's lack of commitment to the Lord Jesus is due to their warped view of the character of God. If we have in any way contributed to that distortion, whether by ignorance, or disobedience to revealed truth, we need to acknowledge it to those people— explaining which facets of God's character were misrepresented by our lives. *"This is the one I esteem: he who is humble and contrite in spirit, and trembles at my word"* (Isaiah 66:2b). Our broken and contrite spirits are a powerful factor that God uses to help bring about contrition in those for whom we are praying.

FASTING AND PRAYER

Since fasting and prayer are often linked together in Scripture with powerful results, we need to be obedient to God's promptings in this regard. Always remember that it's not our fasting that impresses God, only our obedience. The young women at a YWAM School of Evangelism in Switzerland where I was teaching were directed one day by God to fast and pray throughout the day for their unconverted brothers. Remarkable results followed, as some of the girls soon heard about their brothers' conversions.

We can expect to be prompted by the Holy Spirit at times to fast and pray concerning special burdens God puts upon our hearts. In Matthew 6:6 Jesus said, "...*when you pray,*" in verse 2 He said, "...*when you give*" and in verses 16 and 17 He said, "...*when you fast.*" Jesus' repeated use of the word "when" implies that praying, giving, and fasting are acts of obedience that Jesus requires of his disciples.

SPIRITUAL WARFARE

The Bible makes it very clear in 1 John 5:19b (RSV) that the "*whole world is in the power of the evil one,*" but Jesus said, "*I have overcome the world*" (John 16:33b), and God's power is infinitely greater than Satan's. This means that when we pray for the lost, we need to take our stand against the enemy regularly, and command him in the all-powerful name of the Lord Jesus Christ to retreat from them and loose his grip from their spirits, minds, souls, and bodies.

Quote the Word of God, which is our sword in spiritual warfare. The following verses are very powerful as we exercise faith in the power of the written Word:

"*The reason the Son of God appeared was to destroy the devil's work*" (1 John 3:8b).

"*And they overcame [Satan] by the blood of the Lamb, and by the word of their testimony; and they loved not their lives unto the death*" (Revelation 12:11 KJV).

"*I will build my church; and the gates of hell shall not prevail against it*" (Matthew 16:18b KJV).

"*...whatever you bind on earth will be bound in heaven, and whatever you loose on earth will be loosed in heaven*" (Matthew 18:18b).

We must always realize that no matter how difficult or how seemingly hopeless or resistant

14

the unconverted people are, we are not fighting them. We are fighting the enemy, who is our opponent. *"For we wrestle not against flesh and blood, but against the principalities, against powers, against the rulers of the darkness of this world, against spiritual wickedness in high places"* (Ephesians 6:12 KJV).

Satan doesn't give up his victims without a fight. Our warfare is often like a wrestling match. The victory is seldom won in the first round, or necessarily in the second or third. Persistence is necessary in order to win.

We need to constantly remind Satan that *"greater is he [the Lord Jesus] that is in [us] than he that is in the world [the devil]"* (1 John 4:4b KJV). "Therefore," let us tell him, "someone has to lose in this battle, and it's not going to be us." Declare this in faith enough times, and the devil will start believing you and will finally give up. That's been my experience, anyway. I have told Satan that while ever there is breath in my body, I'll fight him by the power and strength of the Holy Spirit for the lost souls for whom I'm particularly burdened, so he might as well quit now. We can then ask God to frustrate Satan's plans in the lives of the people for whom we are praying, and then believe for divine intervention.

THE REVELATION OF GOD'S CHARACTER

Next we should pray that God will reveal to the lost souls the absolute reasonableness of surrendering their wills to the Lord Jesus by giving them understanding of His character. Only God knows of which facets of His character the unsaved have a distorted view. Ask

God to use any means to correct that distortion, and believe that He will.

Ask God to reveal Himself to them in personal ways that they cannot refute, and bring them to the realization that by becoming a Christian they have everything to gain and nothing to lose. Follow this closely by praying that God will bring them to an end of themselves, that everything they are doing to pursue fulfillment outside the pursuit of Him will turn sour and only produce frustration and emptiness. We don't need to make suggestions to the One who is ingenious in His creativity and infinite in His wisdom and knowledge. He has limitless ways that we have neither heard, nor thought of, to answer our prayers.

Now we can ask God to put the fear of the Lord upon those lost souls and restrain them from evil. *"through the fear of the Lord a man avoids evil"* (Proverbs 16:6b). They can be in circumstances of strong temptation, but God can use our prayers to keep them from entering deeper into sin.

THE POWER OF THE WORD OF GOD

"The entrance of Your words gives light; it gives understanding to the simple" (Psalm 119:130 NKJV). We should therefore pray that God will bring His Word to the unsaved, or take them to His Word and give them a desire to read it. God has numerous ways of answering that prayer. Just believe that He will. Derek Prince, a doctor of philosophy, was converted without human instrumentality through reading

the Word of God, and later became an international Bible teacher.

Some of the people for whom we are praying have been exposed to a lot of truth and have hardened their hearts to it. We need to cry out for God to release His mercy to them. Mercy is not getting what we deserve. Moses pleaded for God's mercy for the children of Israel and God answered his prayer. The Israelites' disobedience, rebellion, unbelief, and murmuring certainly deserved God's judgment, but Moses' prayers stayed God's hand of judgment and released His arm of mercy. It is an enormous privilege today to play the same role as an intercessor on behalf of those in similar condition of heart. We can pray, *"In wrath remember mercy"* (Habakkuk 3:2b).

THE PRAISE OF FAITH

To be praying at the deepest level of faith, we can ask God to quicken some Scriptures to us that will encourage us to keep on believing that He is working regardless of what we may or may not see. 2 Chronicles 6:30b says, *"...you know his heart (for you alone know the hearts of men)."*

God can see whether or not the people we are praying for are walking towards the Lord Jesus. He knows whether or not they are softening towards Him and desiring to turn away from their present way of living. If this is so, He will want to encourage us from His Word, as we seek Him. Consequently, it becomes easier for us to enter into the praise of faith. We picture these people as God will make them: "new creatures in Christ Jesus," filled with His love, manifesting the life of Christ. We then praise God wholeheartedly that He is working and that He will accomplish it.

A young woman who attended one of the schools of evangelism where I was teaching had been totally cut off by her parents because she had become a Christian. Her parents had ceased to communicate with her, and she had no idea where they were. She heard me teach on the praise of faith, which was powerfully quickened to her by the Holy Spirit. She began praising God daily in faith for her parents' salvation. Within weeks, her parents were marvelously converted and had made contact with her. Such is the power released through praise.

Since we don't know which of these prayer principles God will use to bring about the conversions of those for whom we pray, let's use them all.

There are times when we are particularly burdened for the welfare of the unconverted and the circumstances are outside of our control or ability to help them. To have peace of mind, we need to put Psalm 37:5 (RSV) into action: *"Commit your way to the Lord; trust in him, and he will act."* The Hebrew word for "commit" literally means "to throw." We "throw" the ones for whom we are concerned at God, asking only that He act to bring the greatest glory to His name in their circumstances.

God is all-powerful, has the knowledge of all that is knowable, has all wisdom, is totally righteous and just, and is all loving. Therefore, He has the ability to catch those we throw at Him, knows how to work on them for their best interests, knows the best methods and timing, will do

only the right and just things by everyone concerned, and longs to catch them. Love's arms
hate to be empty!! God then promises to act.
We believe His Word. Miraculous peace follows.

GOD'S SOVEREIGNTY AND MAN'S FREE WILL

God has given man free will, and that is a
fixed law that will not be violated. However,
through our interceding according to God's
ways, His hand is moved to bring influences and
pressures to bear upon the people for whom we
are praying.

As we persist in prayer and pray tenaciously
like Jesus exhorts us to do in Luke 11:5-8 and
18:2-8, there comes a time when the unconverted find it easier to yield their lives to the Lord
than to hold out against Him. This is what
Elijah meant when he prayed for the fire to fall
on the water-drenched altar on Mount Carmel
in front of the prophets of Baal and the people
of Israel. *"Answer me, O Lord, answer me, so
these people will know that you, O Lord, are God,
and that you are turning their hearts back again"*
(1 Kings 18:37).

In Psalm 33:15 (RSV) the psalmist has the
same thought when he says that God *looks down
from heaven and "...fashions the hearts of them all,
and observes all their deeds."* What an awesome
privilege and opportunity to be able to cooper-
ate with God in "fashioning the hearts of men"
through the wonderful ministry of intercession.

Our spiritual ambition for the extension of
God's kingdom will be manifest by the way in
which we pray for the lost. We can be satisfied
with praying just for their conversion, or we

can pray that they will be converted and become deeply committed disciples of the Lord Jesus. We can pray that they will have a burning desire to know God and make Him known and impact their generation in the power of the Holy Spirit. We can pray that from their steps of obedience to revealed truth, they will be among the overcomers as described in the book of Revelation and be a part of the Bride of Christ.

You may be thinking, "I don't have enough of a burden for lost souls like you're describing to motivate me to pray to this extent." Dear reader, that's okay. But you can take hold of God and ask Him to give you that burden, and refuse to let Him go until He does.

Don't be discouraged if you don't receive a quick answer. You're asking for something of great value. God may test you to see how much you really want to share some of His heart for the lost. When He sees that it's of the utmost importance to you, He surely will answer you. And intimate friendship with God will increase.

GIVE GOD ALL THE GLORY

Finally, it is of paramount importance to tell God that when our prayers are answered, we understand that it wasn't our praying or our fasting or our diligence that caused the miracle of new birth in another. It was because of His grace, His mercy, His power, and His love. We need also to remind ourselves of the part others, perhaps many others, have played through prayer. *"Not to us, O Lord, not to us but to your name be the glory, because of your love and faithfulness"* (Psalm 115:1).

Suggested Prayer

Dear God,

Thank You for making it clear that no one is beyond the reach of Your unfathomable love and unending mercy. Enlarge my heart by making it more like Yours towards the lost. Increase my faith to persevere in prayer for those who are still resistant to You.

By Your grace, I choose to pay whatever price You ask, that precious lost souls may come into Your kingdom. Give them and me a far greater revelation of what You're really like. I believe that is our greatest need. Thank You that You will.

In Jesus' name, Amen.

Other titles by Joy Dawson...

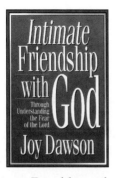

Intimate Friendship with God

Powerfully motivates the reader to fulfill the Biblical conditions for intimate friendship with "the most exciting Being in the universe...Lover-God."
ISBN 0-8007-9084-7

Some of the Ways of God in Healing

Joy is ruthless in her pursuit of truth on the subject of healing. Truth itself heals. All-out integrity in the probing of Scripture on the subject.
ISBN 0-927545-14-4

The Character of the One Who Says "Go"

In this booklet, Joy deals with focused intercession and the character of God. This is foundational material for every Christian.
ISBN 0-927545-08-X

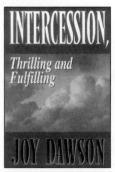

Intercession, Thrilling and Fulfilling

Do you desire: rapid spiritual growth? a ministry that shapes nations? to be free from the guilt of prayerlessness? This book will lead to the fulfillment of these desires and more!
ISBN 1-57658-003-2